The Adventure of Hudson and Clover

ISBN 979-8-89112-270-3 (Paperback)
ISBN 979-8-89112-271-0 (Digital)

Covenant Books
11661 Hwy 707
Murrells Inlet, SC 29576
www.covenantbooks.com

The Adventure of Hudson and Clover

Baltimore and Ohio Railroad

Rosene Wenger

One day, high up in the Appalachian Mountains, two wolf pups, Hudson and Clover, were out playing, running, and jumping around when they came upon the Wise Old Wolf Cave.

Hudson, being the curious pup he is, wanted to go into the dark cave to play.

"No, Hudson, we aren't allowed in there."

"Aww, but come on, Clover. Wise Old Wolf isn't here."
So as fast as he could, Hudson ran into the cave.

"Hudson, come back here," Clover started yelling as she ran into the cave after him. "Hudson, where are you?"

"Boo!" Hudson jumped out at Clover. "I knew you couldn't resist following me in here. You're just as curious as I am."

"I am not," Clover said, "I'm just trying to keep you out of trouble."

As they walked through the cave, they noticed all these pictures floating past them. All of a sudden, the cave started spinning around and around.

"What is happening?" the pups said, looking at each other scared. Then all sudden, the dark black cave came to a stop, and there they stood surrounded by a big crowd.

They heard a deep voice say, "Good afternoon, people of Baltimore."

"Baltimore?" Hudson said with a confused look at Clover. "We don't live in Baltimore. We live in Appalachian Mountain."

They heard the voice said, "We are gathered here today, July 4, 1828."

"What is going on?" Clover asked Hudson.

Hudson looked at Clover. "Shhh, listen, sis."

"To witness the first railroad track to be laid by Charles Carroll." The pups wiggled their way through the crowded area to the front where Charles was.

"Excuse me, Mr. Charles," Hudson said as Charles Carroll turned around.

"Well, hello, Hudson and Clover," Charles said as he patted them on the head.

Shocked, the pups asked, "How do you know who we are?"

With a wink of an eye and a wiggle of his nose, he chuckled. "I've been waiting for you."

"Waiting for us?" asked the pups together. The wolf pups were now really confused.

"Yes, to help you two start your adventure on learning how the railroad started," said Charles.

"Sounds like a lot of fun," the pups said with excitement. "So who are you and what are we doing here?" the pups asked.

DECLARATION
INDEPENDENCE

"I'm Charles Carroll. I'm the last surviving signature of the Declaration of Independence and you have just witnessed the first railroad track being laid."

"Where you and I are standing will be the Baltimore and Ohio Railroad, the first railway for freight and passengers. These rails will go from Baltimore to Sandy Hook, Maryland, which is connected with Harpers Ferry by boats."

Clover looked puzzled. "Why was the railroad created?" she asked.

"Well," Charles said, "by building this railroad, we can trade with the West just like New York is doing, but instead of using the Erie Canal, we would use the train."

"Oh, what is trading?" Hudson asked.

"Well, trading is how we can get supplies that we need like food, crops, and materials. But with the train, not only can we trade with the West, but it's a source to travel faster than by horse. Baltimore Ohio Railroad will be the first freight and passenger railroad in the country. And one day, this railroad will link thirteen great states with the nation.

"Wow, how exciting!" said Clover.

"What was the very first engine?" asked Hudson.

"Oh, that is a good question," said Charles. "It was a Peter Cooper Tom Thumb steam engine."

"What else makes railroading so important?" asked Clover.

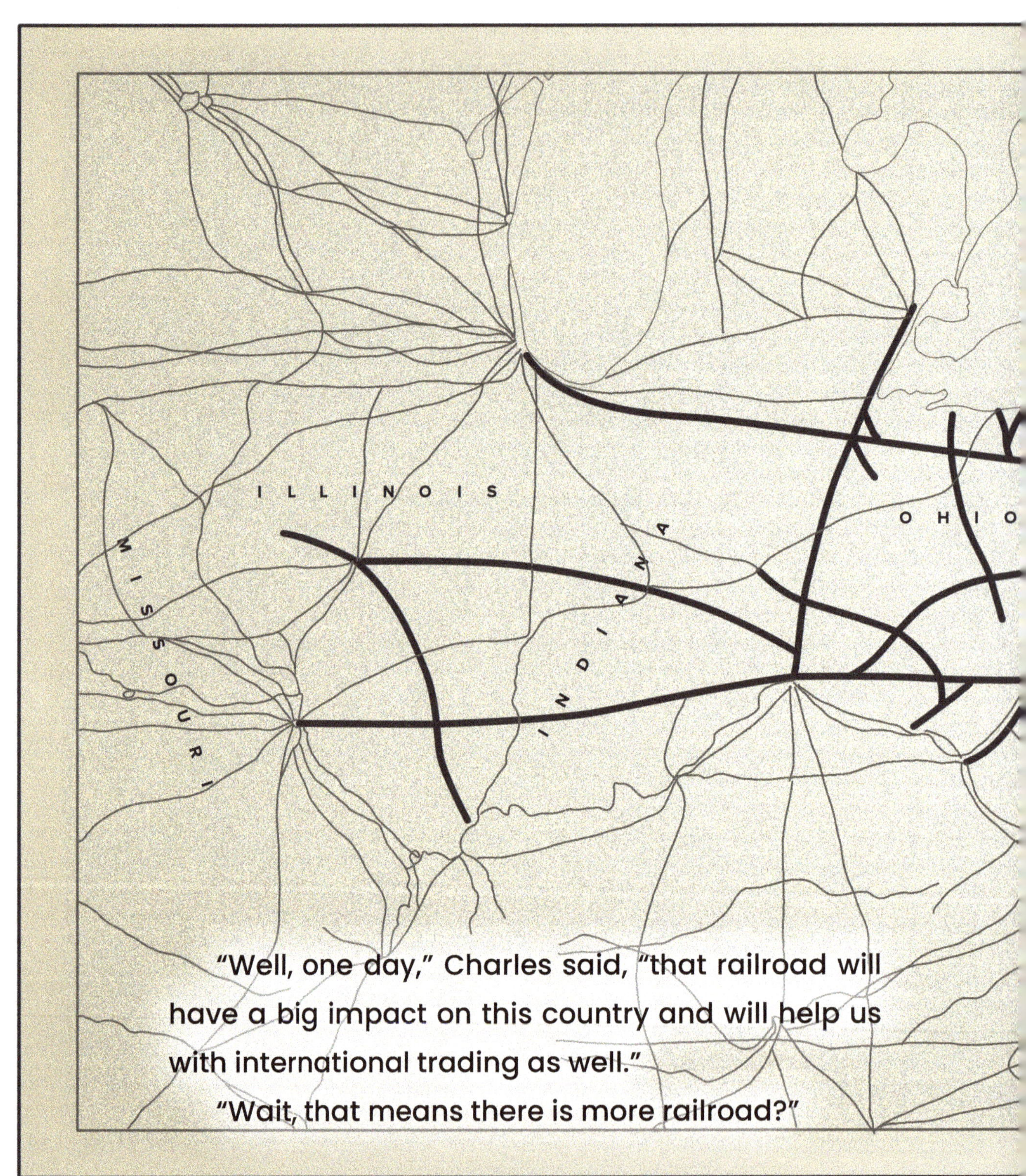

"Well, one day," Charles said, "that railroad will have a big impact on this country and will help us with international trading as well."

"Wait, that means there is more railroad?"

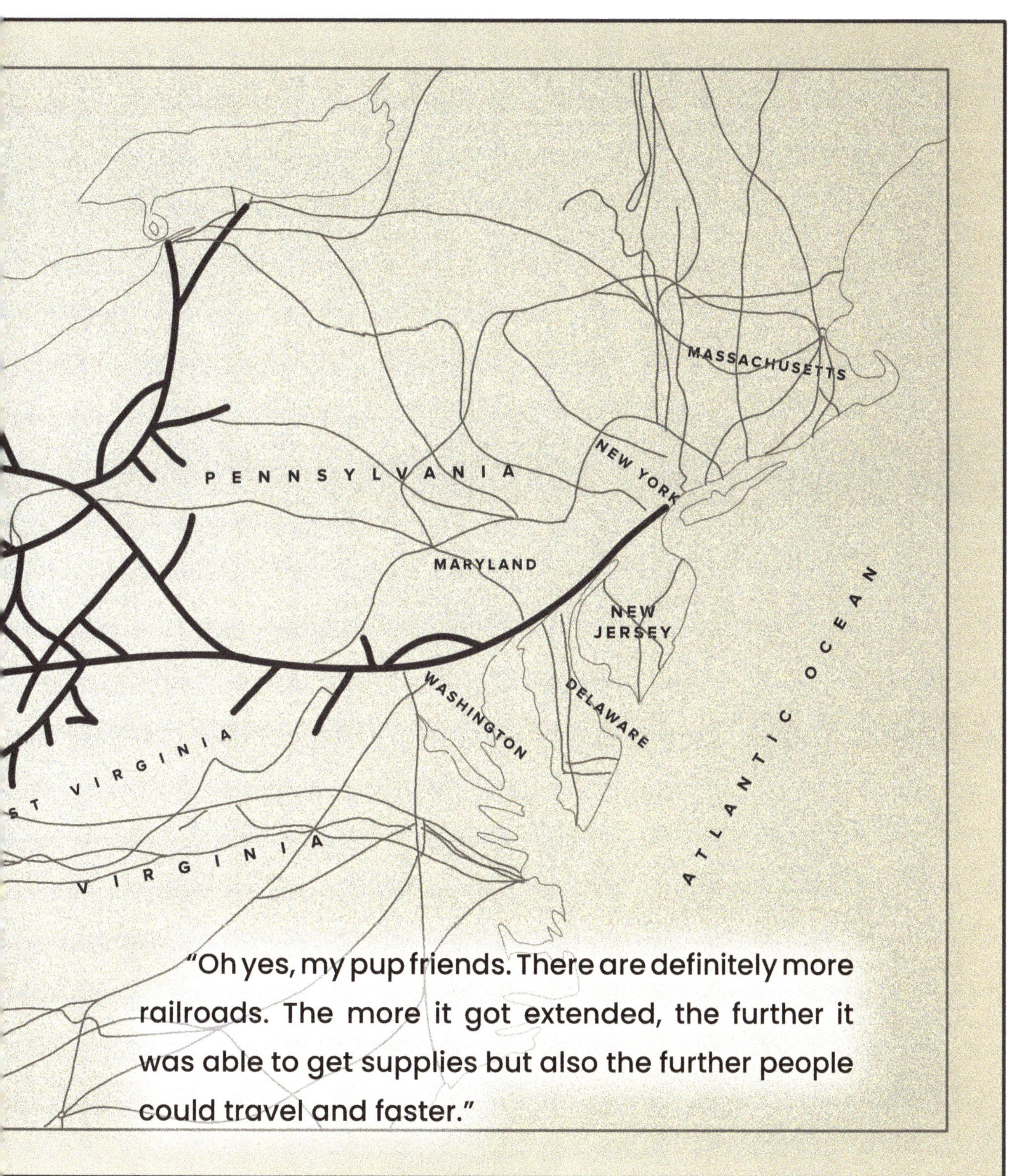

"Oh yes, my pup friends. There are definitely more railroads. The more it got extended, the further it was able to get supplies but also the further people could travel and faster."

"Wow, the railroad was important to the country."

"Oh yes, just like God has plans for us he also has plans for our country."

*****

"Hudson and Clover, dinnertime!"

"Oh no, it's Mom. We have to get going. It was so nice to meet you," said the pups.

"It was nice to meet you too," Charles replied. Charles winking as he say goodbye to the pups as they are walking back into the cave.

"See, aren't you happy you followed me into the cave?" Hudson told Clover.

She looked at her brother and said, "I told you I couldn't let you have all the fun."

As they came out from the cave, they heard yet another voice.

"So did you learn anything today, Hudson and Clover?" They looked at each other. It was the Wise Wolf. The Wise Wolf looked at them. "Well, did you learn anything interesting today?"

"Oh yes, we did," the pups said together.

"Good."

"Hudson and Clover, where are you two?"

"Oh no, Mom! Sorry, Wise Old Wolf, we have to go dinnertime.

"Goodnight, my pup friends."

"Goodnight to you too, Wise Old Wolf."

About the Author

Rosene Wenger and her husband have three kids. They grew up with a railroad in their area and got to ride on it as kids. Now Rosene gets to work there as her job, and their kids get to enjoy riding on the same rails as they did. Their family are followers of Christ, and their lives and their story is a testimony of his love for us.